Daily crumbs poetry

Anna Cellmer

daily emotions on the way of my internal life

Daily Crumbs poetry
by Anna Cellmer

Welcome on my pages and please contact me any time you need it ☺

annaela3@gmail.com

http://stores.lulu.com/annaela3
https://www.facebook.com/pages/Daily-Crumbs-poetry-collections-by-Anna-Cellmer/152073201656457
https://www.facebook.com/opengatesbyAnnaCellmer
https://www.facebook.com/pages/Beautiful-Stranger-by-Anna-Cellmer/211403929016220
https://www.facebook.com/soundofsilencebyannacellmer
https://www.facebook.com/anna.cellmer

All Rights Reserved
Copyright Anna Cellmer 2014

This collection as previous ones are dedicated to a special man that I met on my way and who stay inside me till today and also I wish to thank my special fellows on the way as the wolf and the poet and my dearest Christopher who visit my world after years, seen this collection and helped with edition so it is ready now to give you dear reader

Thank you all who become close to my heart thank you my kindred spirits on the way

You hit me sweetly

I am still watching
You
Wolfie boy
With this sex behind your teeth
And your golden words
Hidden in your swollen mouth
Always ready to hit
You look good
To me

He is listening

You talk like lovers do
You fill this gape
I hold on among the space
When my man is silent
Listening behind the doors
If I still make love

I am just reading you
It's almost the same though

Just more quiet
I devour you
In peace
Secretly

I'll wait

I wish to end up with you this one I know and I dream about
In mean time it seems I do understand the situation we are put in
So I accept this different form we wear now
Yet even then
I can't stop myself
To be in touch with you
In words in pictures in whatever that comes
To share with you
I love this sweet addiction
And I learn how to be patient too
Or how to touch you enough
To bring you closer at times
But I know we need some breaks
And I know we can survive like this
Just in head just right here
Somehow I believe in this
And I'll wait
Deep inside
Because I know
How you make me feel
When you are near
And I know I am good for you
In each little thing you are looking for
I want to be this one
So I am
As you are
This the best man
For me
And this faith keeps me smiling baby

Let's go on

Don't be angry beautiful
We all have our own story to tell
Just sometimes we stop
To look, to give, to take
Or just to enjoy each others company

The way is long
There is so many days to fulfill
Still

We can even go hand in hand
Some time

Or you can have me
The way you wish

Especially in your dreams
This is free zone and I do enjoy

Your visions
Mr. Wolf

Layers and the tree

Layers
Levels of confidence between us

We never cover up the same way to all
doing it piece by piece
Just as we feel as we want
To let someone else
To come closer
To know you
To become a part of the story
You live in

I see you all are sitting
On the branches
Some so high others lower a bit
I am so happy you are here
My sweet friends
My birds

The centre

Where is the centre?

Here
It's you

Yes you
You are the centre

And all the action is around
Or in you

And you are on the way
From understanding to creation
Of your own life

It's nothing wrong to be in love a bit
I think
Or showing this or that
To someone you like
If you enjoy it

To Narcissus

I like you little Narcissus
You are as shy as me
We play here as two children
Using words
Like others use their hands and eyes
Or the rest of things they have

Just thoughts you are

So not real people you are
Just thoughts on the screen
Some make me feel good some touched
But there is nothing behind
Nothing real, material
Thoughts are alright
But somehow it's sad
You do not really exist
For me
So you can disappear

Will I cry?
I don't know
Mind is a lot
To build a day
And the day is all that I really have

So yes I will cry, then I will forget

We never really touch never really exist here
We are nothing but hidden dreams
We can flow with the wind or stay here
In this world of illusions
And this is alright yet somehow sad too

It's hard to explain
Why so disappointed I am now
I will be fine soon I'll be all right

Let's forget it

Is this true
Did I push you away for good?
All my lovely spirits here
Who enjoyed this being together
This special kind of trust
This journey through wonder land
This smile among the space
This little romance

Do you feel hurt now?
All is spoiled destroyed somehow?
Do you really feel like this?
Is it all my fault indeed?

Yes I was a bit angry on you
yes disappointed a bit too
Though it's ok
Emotions fly away
And this what stay is nothing but smile again
Though maybe a bit more calm maybe not so open wide
Yet still smile for you and because you are here
Because we know how to enjoy each other too
So don't feel so bad anymore
and stay
It's ok
Let's be as we are
It doesn't matter
What I tried to show you
You don't understand me well
So forget
And let's smile as before
Nothing really happened
This little drama just ended

Let's forget
Let's forget
I love you all as you are
Don't be afraid
Don't feel sad
You are ok

Me and Island

I think I like this Desert Island I chose to live in
With few eyes which keep watching my dreams
And this one heart I love to believe in and cherish here
Yes and these few minds and spirits I love to feel near me
I am used to this through years and I am not sure
There is something else I could enjoy more
Oh maybe just your touch again and your voice
and your smile of course
But it's still just the Island I live in
and
It's you
Who came
Nothing else

Awareness

Growing up
Is just to put off another barrier you had inside as a child
To free away your soul
From each rule
That others give to control your moves
Through the world

The more free you are inside
Then more of your steps
Are made by your own will
And more enjoyable they are
And more clear

And you can smile more
Aware
Because you know
That you can do whatever you want
From now

He and you

I am sorry to say so
But you are nothing but a jealous man
With spirit not big enough
To believe in this love
And in human as well
You believe in your god instead
And it's good for you
But you are not bad enough
To understand my soul so good
As he do

Me and poet

You seem to be cruel and honest enough
To get my attention and respect

Me and my man

You may lead me to good and to bad as well
And it doesn't matter
Where we go
It's just your charm I feel
Nothing more

My demented dark attraction

You seem to know well what attracts a woman as me
I wonder where and how we can follow each other here
Yes you are special to me and I do enjoy your die-hard mind
I feel comfortable and familiar within its horny sight

I'll read you more
If you let me do so
It's delicious thing to eat and to live for

Fellows in a dream land

Some of us have very special dreams
Like you and me
Here
and there

Delightful

There is no other Power
I can believe any more
Except
This sweet one hidden
In your lips and palms
Leading me
To the real pleasure
And forgiveness

The Birth

From the first day
I came to this world
I know
What I am living for

It's how we've found each other

In this ocean
Of differences
It's so good
To find
Another Island
Of similarity

Yang Ing

It's so good
To find each other
Now we can build
Our heaven and hell
Our castle and immortality
On the island of our dreams and reality

Did you come to save me?

Nice to see you again
Wolf man
I know you're just passing on
My desert land
But we both know
There are some dreams
That we could give
To each other
We can smell them
In the sight
Of our footsteps

You know

It's you who are my man for good
It's you who I belong to
It's you who I really want

All other dreams
Fulfill me still
To make me
Perfect one
You can drink every night
And feel enough delight
To never stop
And to live for this
Only

We missed at night

I am just afraid my darling man
That when I dream of you
You can come in mean time
And I wont even notice
You were here
To devour me sweetly
For real
I fell asleep
And you unable
To take my soul with you
As you love
So disappointed you can be
This way
My beloved

Time to go far a bit

I am not another sheep in your garden my friend
Nor the flower which you love to watch and smell so much
I am free now and I don't need any herd man
I need my wolfish dark angel now to play with
I need him to fulfill the wildest dreams
And to spoil me or to save me
I need his power to live still
And to give

So it's time to go far a bit
We have different needs inside
So we can't walk hand in hand

Another trip to favorite city

Soon she will walk again
Through the passage of her entire dream
How it's sweet

I love to belong to you

If you only know how wonderful is to belong to you
You wouldn't say such silly things like this
I'll never have enough of you
My beloved
Whatever you do to me
Whatever you say or let me do to you
I'll always ask for more
I'll be grateful
That you came that you enjoyed me
Again
Even if I'm not always able to do all
As you say so
But I try and I do enjoy
Your sweet imaginative mind
And all this charm
Between us and all this love

My dream and me

How do you think
We can be friends still
If you wish to kill my dream
Don't you know
I do not exist without it?
You can kill me the same
It's not any difference for me
Life without him
Is nothing

The reason

I need to be with you
Because
You are the one
I am able to fly with
And flying
Is the one thing
I really enjoy
In this world

Why

You ask me why
Not only you and him
Well as you know
In each story
We need more plots to enjoy

Besides they are only slaves of mine
You are my master and slave in one
That's why
Forgive me my nature and this charm
I still splash to them somehow
Soon it all can disappear
When I close my book
When I stop to breath
By love
By you

So for now I just enjoy
What life has to offer to me
But it's you who are my dear love
I wish to drown for good and forget the world

Why too

So you disappeared again
That's why baby
I need to keep all around
To survive
With this wonderful you
Within my world but
Without you inside and beside me
Most days that I live here

Now

I know that situation doesn't look good
You were wonderful as always you
And I was in heaven
For this little moment in space again
To be now where I am

And I still feel this real light
Only when you are beside
Even if now
There is no you so suddenly
Without any warning without any word

What happened?
My love
Where are you?

Don't you remember that I live for you?
What to do now?

I don't believe in any doubts
From all around
I know I saw you and felt your touch your sight your love
You must be for me still
You just disappeared
But it can't be for long
I don't believe that you have been gone

Selfishness

We are so selfish in love
Only because I feel it to you
I wish that you look at me and see me
The same way I see you
So perfect, so beautiful
The best one for me
Whatever you do
Yes I wish to believe you see the same in me
Because I know that you love
You showed this to me not even once
And I remember this and I will be
So selfish as I am still.

Humans

Yes men are not perfect
And we can lose them suddenly
That's why they are so beautiful
And we have to enjoy each special moment
That comes with them and goes too

Touches

The right touch

And I show you how much love is inside me
How deep you can go and it seems there is no end to it

The wrong touch

And I am not here anymore

So you live

Emergency you said
Well at least you live
Good to hear
Bad boy still
How do you suppose I could share life with you
If you just leave me like this

So I see nothing has changed
Things come and go
As this short slight attraction we build
At times we meet
Just to keep it for long
But how about every day?
Are you sure it'd work this way?

Calm down

I think you don't want too caring
and needy me in your life
So I calm all emotions down
Let's forget about each other for a week or more
And live our lives just
As we never existed
As we never have met

Yes let's try like this
Life still has its charm
Even when you are not around

Do I believe in this now?
Well I try
I don't need to fly high
All the time
So I calm down

Turning into the dream of life
Or simple things I have here
I can do them with a smile still
So it's true it's just the mind
That lets us feel so good or so bad
We can create peace inside as well
Yes
For how long?
Just as it is needed I suppose
To the next time
You are around

You and death

Yes I know about your fascination with death
But for me at least in this particular moment in time
It's nothing but the end of the journey
And I am more interested
How to fulfill each day I still have
Than to explore this that I don't believe
Is something more
Than rest
So forgive me I won't follow you here
We can meet again when you are thirsty for life
Which you can squeeze from my lips or other things I hide
Or show depends
On the time, my mood, and your talents

Nothing else...

There is nothing else I wish to be
Than the beauty you have in your dreams
And you long for in the morning

Free again

I think that you are not ready yet
For this relationship to build anything real
I feel free then
To take all that this life gives to me
Still
I know you are near
It's enough for me

Time to go our separate ways

Is there any life outside of you?
Can I still enjoy all things around?
Well I hope
Because I don't feel you are beside me
For real

I have to live myself
Yes these moments with you
I can't compare to anything I had so far

Yes this is real love

But maybe
I can live still
Having you as a memory and little dream

When there is no need in you
To be with me for real
I have to go now I think

And to try to have fun in this life still
Love for you is not all I can enjoy
In this world
I hope

I won't beg you to be mine
All the time
It doesn't work

It's not attractive to you
And it's tiring for me
To live just by illusions

You share from time to time
To feed my dreams and to keep me still

Ready for you
And full of love

It's just not enough

Maybe all you want
Is to keep me still

Who knows?

Maybe it was even part of your plan
To let me leave you alone for good this time
So you have what you want
Freedom
I hope you will enjoy this more
Than this me and you
Together

You and he

And again you talk to me
Like you were him

As you were living inside his mind
Whispering all this...he wish to tell me
And I wake up
To your words
As to love
I still feel to him

Amazing connection
of three minds or more
I don't know
I just feed my soul
By your love

You and your bloody poetry

Some men who write poetry seem a bit infantile
To me
but not you
You are really wild
Bony cruel mad sick
That's what I like in it
You bad boy fascinated in these things
That normal people are scared to think

Yes I like men like you
Who do it so gently
This charming diving into the madness we can be in
Ignoring rules, borders, purity

Yet still so shy
With relation between
You and me
It's somehow sweet

Independence

Little secret room with all useful stuff
Some clothes, books, PC
For a couple of days staying
In my favorite place in the world
Few times a year

With you coming there
When I let you know
That I am
And I wait you

Recent dream
I have
About me and you
Independently together though

It is still for me

I am here
For all those never written poems
I can feel in the memory
Of your kisses

I wonder how many lives
I can have at the same time
Still being myself in this
It seems that at least two
Just as we are
Right now

Exception

I hate anyone who tells me what to do
Except you
You are cute even in this
And I am glad to listen
You
It's always the part of this sweet game
We play
Even not being aware
To the end
We create
Another day
In our play

Where could I find something more
Beautiful?

Where could I drown
So blissful?

I don't know
I never found
Anything more exceptional

So far

And years go by

Some years we are together here
And I still have a feeling
That it's just the beginning
Are we going so slowly or is this way so long?
Who cares
Anyway I love this
No end between you and me
This endlessly
This dream

So I am here
and you are too

I hope

It's enough to dance still
It's enough to live
and love

Power

I love to give you power
Over my body and soul
Because I love you and I trust you enough
To know that
You won't use it
In any other way
Than to make me smile even more
At the end and more open for you
As I ever thought that I could

It's the most wonderful thing
I ever felt
and it's good

Love is for these who are able to survive

We are so easy to touch
This jealousy of love is impossible
It lets only the strongest one survive
All the rest have to leave this boat
Before they do something wrong
or drown too deep to still live and sing
Her song

Something you can't do

You can't simply kill this dream I live for
Having nothing to offer instead of

Please try to understand
My silly friend
How important this faith is for me
When nothing else lets me feel
So good as this one last thing
I still believe in

It's dangerous to take away
My own soul from me
Giving me few empty caresses
To get excited
It's much too little for me
When I know
How good I feel when I believe
In love

This last little thing
Which is the reason to live
For me

A future

Future
It doesn't matter
When right now
Right here
I feel eternity
In this little message
You keep
To send still

and heaven is in me

Constancy fits to you

I thought it is also a jealousy
That keeps us so close so tightly
But it was before
Now I can find so much joy
When you tell me
You are not interested in any girl but me
This makes you more attractive now
Even when I do tease you
All the time
Making hell for your mind
How I love when after that
You still say to me
My Darling

It's all I want to hear and live for
To hear
These words
From your mouth
Whatever I have done
Before

I love to be your bitch, your whore
Just don't leave me any more

Romance

I like the fact
That you are not afraid of death
If it comes
From my hand

Distant lover

You always just let me
Be
Hungry for you more
And it works

All I have so far
Is this desire
For more you
Inside my world
And my hole

Wrong steps

I do all that I shouldn't do
Looking for general laws or directions

but I still feel your breath
beside me
maybe it's just a dream
but sweet still

so I keep
drifting
in thoughts
into your world
opening my secrets to you
with this hope

that it's not too much for you
and you rather stay silent
than you say go
because you can't stand me
anymore

You must believe you hold a key

You are the one I gave the key
Into my world
I hope you do not destroy
What you hold

I am not sure
I'd be able to enjoy it still
If I don't have you
You who can do whatever
You want

How I wish you could be excited at least
Once or two
Or in tears or in smiles
Just looking at me
From inside my dreams
And sins

It should be amusing
A bit at least
I think...

Wisdom of lover

I think that you perfectly know
When I am totally yours
And when I look around
For little dessert
I could taste
mean while

Of our story

You are too smart sometimes
My beloved
But that's why

I do

adore

You

So much

Not words you need

So many useless words
I gave to you again
If only one you really need
Is the picture of my ass
Dancing slowly beside your eyes

To let your hungry hands
Move closer to it
And to play
And to hold

This

What you really want
To taste
To take
To talk to

Making your cock so hard
And your mind so wild

Just as I love
It can be
For me
When we meet
In darkness
Of our unfulfilled dreams
Still

Confession

So you have it
You have it all
With details
My love
And what now?

You know how I am afraid
What you can feel
What you can say

I am guilty
I know
Could you forgive me please?
And don't let me go?

I wish to stay
Inside your world

Just let me in
I wait so long
I know I was so bad
I made so many mistakes
And mess around
But you know
How much I love you
In this
And that it's done
Just because
I feel you are so far
At times
And I am weak enough
To do wrong things
Especially from the time
I see you are able to enjoy this
So please
Let me live
Beside you still
I want this
I need this
And I dream
Is it enough
To forgive?
All sins?
Please let me believe still
In our dreams
Don't let them gone with the wind
We need them still
Both I hope
My beloved

You just fight again

All good now
I can believe still
You are wonderful and mine
Just as always in fight
With all real problems this life put on you
You never share too much of them
You always want to give me the best

My man how beautiful you are
How sexy
You don't even know
How much I adore you
And the fact you are so good
But you never try to show this

You are for me just this sweet sexual beast
And beautiful lover
For my pleasure and for relief

Lets stay in dreams my love
It's the best space for both

A request

Just tell me
When you stop your love for me
So I know the date
of my death

Too little still

Precious moments
Why do we have to wait for them so long again
What to do in mean time, my man?
Cry, think of it, miss
Or try to replace somehow
This special charm
We had once upon a time
And believe?
It's still too little
For me to live
To not feel this waste
Of the time

I do feel now

In meantime

Love
I learn still how to please you
Reading books of all possible kinds of behaviors people do
Bad or good doesn't matter my love
I just wish to be a good whore
In moments we are together
All the rest of the time
I have fun or wait or love
I know it's hard sometimes to handle
But I try
Why?
To keep my self happy free and wild
Just as I love and you love me to be
I think
or to make you a bit mad
well I am also bad
Just as you like

My dear Marquise de Sade

How I love your dark free mind
I can even agree with the fact
That God is just a dream
We love to feed our minds and hearts
And some of us are wrong
For sure even fools
Anyway dreams are good until they let us be happy I think
Well even if I don't have this one dream anymore
I have another one I love to live for
This one you don't like too
But I do
Maybe because I am not so bad
As those creatures you describe
Monsters inside
Oh god sometimes it's really hard to go through
This madness you write about
Even just to show this philosophy
You love to own yourself

Yes following passions is the thing for me too
But I don't like that you are afraid of love

I prefer to believe in this one good thing
It keeps me mad and alive still and free

Besides I don't dream of hundred priests fucking me hard

Nor about killing children
or other victims of perversity
You love so much to describe
No my friend
I am not free this way I am not going there, what for?
Is it really so wonderful?
Anyway you just like to go through bad things to show something
To amaze to shock of course

I admit I've never met any man as you
And I admire this lack of borders too
Inside your imagination of course
Such a free man you are!
So wild!
Somehow funny too
Master I can say
But such a bad boy!
Shame on you!
I think I should spank you!

But this is what is good
Is to know
That you can do within your mind
Whatever you want
And that even love
Sometimes is better just to keep in your mind in your dream
Than realize all of what you wish

well at least not too fast

You have it still though
Inside you

Oh my love how many times we will be planning to meet
Again and again
And create this story of us
Just to live just to smile
And feel more?

I love this you know?

I love even those never kept promises you make
I know it's hard at times to realize some dreams
Besides they are more beautiful like this
When we long for them still so much
My absent lover
I'll always love you more
Than this one I just touch right now
Yet still I have hope for more
and this is what keeps alive this love
and all charm of life
I suppose

Silly Comparison

People are:
Stupid or smart
Depends how smart we are in fact to say that
Sensitive or not
Depends how sensitive we are if we can see this or feel it somehow
Deep believers in God whatever called or realists
Depends on many things even the time we are actually in
Bad or good
Depends made up of souls, community, beliefs or family or other things happened to us and what is actually bad thing or good?
Generally, culturally, locally, socially, in human eyes, in god eyes or nature?
 Who really knows?
Oh yes we know we create the system already to live by so let's leave this for now.
Funny or serious, oh depends too, from many factors of course
Sexy or not it also depends on this what we like and what we want

Oh actually what is this catalogue for?
We are different that's all
But if we can see some are beautiful and good for us so it's nice
Let's be friends or let's have a little romance
or true love with each other
This is what we can do here just chose and go for it
And live

Yes indeed.

Writers and lovers

With writers and poets
As with lovers
Sometimes it's better
To try them all
Before you decide which one
Fits to you the most

Ps My dear poet friend
I am sorry I read another one more
But you know I'll be back to you soon
So do not worry and write still
If not for me so for them

My dear poet

My dear poet friend
Your influence on my blog site is so evident!
I am so sorry though
To steal another picture from your site
But they fit so well to my mind
And this pleasure from this little crime is so big
So I can't help it...

I know you will forgive me
I don't know about others though
Let's not think of them now
And live as long we can as long as we wish

Oh yes indeed!
Let's live
To the end of love
Of course
Then we can die in peace
With smiles on our face

Slight difference

Strange thing
Sometimes I can't find big difference between
Poets I read here
And lovers I give myself to
I feel the same unfaithful
When I stop with one to start with another

How I love to have my heart open wide for you
Now you can fuck my mind
Even more than you could do this
With my cunt

Proportions

In each life
There is time of passion
As there is time of boredom
There is place for love and hate
There is time for work and rest
And so on

Just proportions
Make some differences
I suppose

Summer wine

Another summer ahead
lets drink some wine
Instead
of other things
we could do
If we were able to move

Flowers instead how nice

Oh I didn't know
You killed your wife
Some time ago
It is so kind of you
To bring flowers on her grave
And give her prayer or two

So she rests now
and smiles to you

You are good boy today
What a nice surprise for her
Do you think she cares?

At least

So you insist
To not let me be so sure
Of you still
Good that at least
At the end
Of my despair
You come to say

This

What I need to hear

To live

Walking shadow

You
A bottomless pit
Where I drink my water
Of dreams
To feed myself
The way I wish

Your silence
Is the most courageous food
For my craves
I still hide before
Blind eyes
Of the crowd

As your words
Are balsam
For all longings
You put me in

To let me want you
More
And to let me
Drift on my way
With more passion

With the little help
Of your assurance

That we belong
To each other
At the end

Imagination

I love to imagine myself
That it is you
Who still look at me

here

Small big things

Sometimes just a second
Is enough that little things
Grow up enough
To kill

Good if you are in time
To pass this short time
And live
And back to normal
Like nothing never happened

And small things are small again
No harm in them

Moments are good yet not enough

Yes some moments in space are wonderful
And still worth to go for
Yet this immortal hope
For eternal joy
Is better

It's like a sweet dream
You can feed each moment
Of your life
And smile inside
The big internal light

Is this what you own
And this makes you rich
As nothing else ever could make it

No one can take it from you too
So you are the king or queen
Of life
And this is what is great
In this
Indeed

Island and cities

Sometimes I live on the desert island
After this I'm back to the cities of thousand lovers who try to reach me
Promising kisses and sweet dreams and cute things I can take going with them

And it's all good until I can reach your island
And you among the crowd

Commandment of love

"And you won't have any gods before me"

I am your goodness
And you are my lord

From now on we can enjoy the world
As it is written in the old book
of love

Curiosity

Is it not too big a crowd
You let me in suddenly to enjoy?

Who knows
For now I am surprised enough
To smile and to agree
Just to try something else a bit
What is behind
And how it can be
With you like this
My sweet?
Again you let me wish
Something more
Than I thought so far
I can do
That is good
Exciting
And complex enough
To drown in it

and to dream still

Into your world

Not too many answers I really need from you
I just enjoy I can dance still
When you are near
With all your world too
That you want me to accept and to love

Maybe it's just because
It's you
Who let me feel this
That I need
Let's dance my love
Still as you wish as you play
And you dream of
This music is good for both
Maybe for three or even more?
Who knows

Let's try for now
What can happen next
Time will show
I suppose

Too many words can spoil this I know

Too many words my darling
I have still too many words
It all doesn't matter
Her reasons
I know

I don't want to spoil this all
Before it comes
Let me stay silent now
You know that I like this
And I do enjoy
Each of your thoughts
So just wait now
Stay calm

Just these smiles inside
You can keep
Your lover is amazing still
So you can live
By this dream

What choice do I have?

So now I have to lie
For your good
What else will you let me do
To keep this love?

Whatever it can be
You know that I will understand
And I will agree

No matter how silly it can be
I will go for it

It's just how it works
Walking by your side

Wherever it leads

Still feels so sweet

When you are in it

My beloved it's still the best way to go

I know it sounds silly and naive

But it is just how it feels

Too much between

But you know
Between you and me
There is still so much of all these things...
That sometimes I just dream
Of simple smiles
And a simple kiss
And that it could
Take longer than these few moments
In space
We can have

Fools

Some people find it so easy to judge others
When they don't know even the little part of the story
They seem to be a blind fools
Who just don't know
How sweet it is and how it is good
To live in your own dream world
No matter what
Oh they make me so angry sometimes
They should rather stay silent
To not make me feel mad

but alright they can all think or say what they want
I just don't need to listen is all

That's why

You ask me why
Special you were for me

Well maybe
It's just this little poet
Inside me
And with you I could feel
This lovely smell of new fresh love in the air
Just when you were beside me

This unwritten story
That could happen between you and me
If we go into each other a little bit more
Maybe if we meet in a bit different time
Hard to say, I just know
It was special
That's all
This sweet little touch
Which I adore

My Mysterious

Life seems so sweet
When you have so special friends
Around

As you right now are for me
You bring smiles
With your gentle understanding sight
Inside my mind

Thank you my mysterious one
You are so wonderful
Friend
Through all this time
But today
You just made my day
Again

And who knows what the future brings
And how many smiles we can share
So I just thought to thank you
For all this that you bring to me
Right now right here

Who you are

Few of you
Are my world
Right now

Some special intimate things

These are things in this world
Which remain beautiful
As long as they are intimate
Between two… let's say few
Just make them public
And they lost their charm
Forever

Mamma Mia!

I promise to never grow up to the end
and to feel as a dancing queen at times too
Every day... and night I wish I could
At least just to stay with my dreams
I promise

And to have some fun
Within my wonderland

In the name of adventure
In the name of special life
Love pleasure desire

Amen

Perfect love story

You just let her do it
Then you let her end it by herself

She just can't stop talking to you
Like you were still here

She can't stop hurting you
Even when you do not care any more
Of all her actions

But she still goes on

Like nothing happened

What did happen by the way?

Action

I know I am bad for you now
But you deserve this
Your lack of care
Is unforgivable
And made me like this

I will think later about consequences
if they exist

Is this so easy?

Amazing
The sun is still shining
The life seems to still keep some light inside me too
Even if you are not around me anymore

How strange
This calmness

I just think how you can feel now
How it is
With you

Yes I am still curious
But this is all I can do
I have done enough
Far too much I guess

Well at least
I know
How it is
To feel all this
We all need

At times
Yes indeed

I know it

Distance

I wonder how far we can go from each other
And if it can be eternal
Just as this love we believed once
That can be true

I don't know

I don't know

Yet this story seems to go on

Somehow

Even when you went out

Sometimes short is better

Yes sometimes when the conversation leads
To nowhere
It's better to stop it

There is no wrong way for a dreamer

Very well this you say
You just don't understand one thing
That I am one of these

Dreamers

And if one day I stop following them
It means
I died

I live only when I come closer to them
I do not hurry up too much
It all comes in the right time
Sometimes a bit unexpected yes
But all of this I can handle
Not losing the sense and the main things
In life

You forget also that without me
All the rest wont be the same
And there is no me without my hope and my dreams
So I have to go where I see the light

That's right

If

If I have you
If I really could have you
Perhaps for sure
I'd not feel you that much
As now
Just when I've lost you

So maybe it's better like this
To keep you here
I know well
How to live with you
Just inside
My own soul

It's better to stay with this ghost
You became for me
Than see how it could be
If you and me were different
or if we met in a different time
And just belong to each other more
Than only in dreams
That are now broken too

You see
We couldn't stand this
For real

So you left

So it really happened
You left

Maybe you are right
I am not worth this pure dirty love
We fell in
Between one and the second dream

Just the way we are

I think you understood
What I am going to do now

And that decision was made a long time ago
It's just time now
To do what I plan to do
From the start

Yes sometimes this plan
Has no sense no right time
But it is still inside
Somehow

So there is no return
I suppose

Just the way
I go
For now

Sometimes only inside
Not so sure
If it is good

But this is the way you are
You can't change much of yourself
You just have to accept and follow
Your way

No matter what people say
You know all answers the best
You just have to listen them
And be brave

Yes
I suppose
Yes

Is it not this that we all love to believe?
At least

Nothing but the heartache

Maybe you are a bit disappointed with this silence now
But how many times can I make myself a fool
In the name of this "love"
That seems to be nothing but illusion of my heart and hopes
I think it is enough for me

Yes it is baby

Moments of truth

At times you feel like you are a bit lost
In all these dreams that lead you through this life
Yet I hope that in the right time you know
This perfect choice
Just when you really feel it
And when you know what you want

Do not spoil these moments of truth
They are really rare
And they are good

5 minutes too late

You are this man
Who I didn't want to do this with
But I did

So now we both have to forget
That it ever happened
Immature you can say I am
Well false signs I gave to you this night
These smiles, a little care, hugs and dance

And these five minutes you asked me to stay in your place
And a few little more things
I guess
Let me do this
Make you so blind insensitive enough
To take me without my permission

Now you have to disappear from my life
Like a ghost from the past
A little scar inside my mind

We didn't really build any story between
It's all misunderstanding I think

And you
Yes you my love
This one who just left me alone
Some time ago
For all these nights

How I wish you could erase this man now
Who just came and took me
So easily
Without my wish or need
To make me feel nothing but disgust
Inside

You should be there
Not he
Do you know this?

Vanity Fair

There is a lot of colours in life to enjoy
In each time you have something to discover and go for
Yet this one is still the most precious for all
No matter where it is found and for how long
Happy are these who know its taste
Unhappy too because anything else
Can't be enough when it is lost
Yet life has still its charms and joys

Of course
Of course

The Gypsy's wife

I just need to go now
To dance and to know
The taste and the smell of this life a little bit more
After all I'll be back
I'll knock on your door
As before
Asking for love
Like a dog
And you will let me come
Because it all was written in this book
We live in
And you accept this
Because you know me enough
To let me dance
Still
I'll be back to you
Or I'll die
Doesn't matter
I had you
So everything now
Is just a bonus
To enjoy
But I did all what I had to do
With you
I did good
All that I could
To feel you
So I go now
To enter the life
More wide

Good bye
For now

A call

So it is real
You do not give a shit for me
At least I know that you live

I feel so piteous
With this
Knowledge
In me

Such a fool again I was here
God why does it have to be so sad
Love is just overrated

So there is nothing more to say
Time to go

You didn't tell me

It seems you forget to tell me
About this one little thing
That you will get married soon
Well good luck
She waited quite long
12 years
Oh amazing we are here 5 too
This time is running so fast
Don't you think so?
Amazing how long we belonged to each other here

I wonder when you decided though?
The same time you promised me this life together forever?
Or recently?
When you suddenly gone after all this mess you prepared for us both?

Any way it is a good decision
I hope you can make it
She is good for you
She will forgive you all
And she won't be as me
I think
She won't hurt you as I can
Playing your own game

We were good as a dream
You can't say it wasn't nice
You belonged to me here
Quite sweetly
Sometimes cruel too but mostly sweet

Yes for sure
Well such a special fantasy
It is a good thing
To live
Isn't it?

Just how to release my mind now
And go to all these who wait
I think the time as always
Is best to forget

And keep your mind and heart free
From this love which doesn't work anymore
Somehow

I don't know even why
And what I did
That you decided to leave
Without single word

We all have its ways I suppose

Anyway she is such a gentle lady
It was nice to talk with her
Last night

Yes good to know
Some facts

Send her my regards
and well I hope you will be all right
I wasn't able to lie to her this time though
Besides you didn't ask

Congratulations again
I am sure you will tell her something clever enough
To make her wish you still
You are such a charming man
When you want to be

And I am as I am

Always too free on my way

Dancing still

Teasing your dreams
Like before
Your sweet little things
To enjoy

Our little play

And see darling
What we have done
A womanizer
Dirty boy
and your naughty bitch and whore

What a beautiful couple

I will miss us now

Who can play the same
As you and me?
And to keep this so innocent still?
Just like a dream
Of perfect love

We had once and we had to lose
Oh you were here too
For sure
At least for some time
My partner in crime

But we went too far
I know
Though
It was worth it

Oh this reality

Oh this bad reality
It always spoils everything
Just why I had to lose you
Even here?

I was too bad again
Or too fast
I started to make too many moves
Into the real world
It scared you away

It has to be too much to gain
Or to lose

I understand now
How mad I am
To believe

It could ever be real

A stone

Why does it seems like you think
That I am just like a stone
And nothing ever can be wrong

So it is easy for you
To go
Like nothing happened

And she will just go on
Her open story
Her empty talk

I'll try as always I'll try
No matter how many tears fall down
In mean time

I'll stay tall
and smiling still
to the end
whatever it brings

That's how I learn to live

All these questions

I think you do not know how much it costs me
To not send you any messages for so long a time
With all new questions I have on and on
Why have you gone?
Do you want me to go?
Don't you love me anymore?
Why did you leave me actually?
Especially when I was so near

I have never felt I can be so far from you
Just when I was almost before your door
So I have done what I have done
And yes I know how it works
How this makes you feel now
Even without telling me this
I know how it feels

Maybe you just need some time
And I give it to you
Or I try to leave
When I don't believe you want me still

Just why I had to do all this
Or to dream
That I can be with you
Even for a while
Like nothing happened
Just like before

When you are fighting right now
To keep your face
Before her eyes
And I know it can be hard
Especially now when she found out
I am here...
In your life in your dream
Hidden so far so deep
For 5 years

Licking wounds

Love is at times as a war
We are licking our wounds right now
Soon another battle can come
Who knows?
Just as in a war
We can expect everything
And we have to go for it
Because we need this

So I stay here
As before
On the scene
Of my private show
For one actor mostly
Sometimes more

Where shall I go?

Incoming birthday wishes

To the chosen one:

I wish you could act as a loving man again
Not like the last asshole
As recently when I was so close

I wish me to not be as a whore
Giving my body to any nice man
Just to make me feel better
At time you are away

But it seems it is not possible
Because I love to keep all these lovely men around
They are only one little thing in this world
That can please me enough
To enjoy this life still
When you are not here
And when I am not sure if you care at all

Besides it is you who showed me
How free I can be
Yes you first
My sweet dirty boy
It's all your fault!
You didn't know I'd love this so much though
So I forgive you

Another thing
I wish you to marry a woman who you can be totally open with
And who you love to fuck so much as you did with me

But I see you have other priorities in your life
That is good and fine
That is right

And I am bad to you enough
Just so much as you
Maybe even more
So go to hell!
My beloved
There is no way for us
Like this

I hate that I still love you
I really do

Fuck you!

Yes I wish so!

And I wish I could stop this show
Somehow

But I can't
I love this madness too much
To give it up
And live my life
Outside

Here is all my heart
Or maybe just a part

Who knows how much?

Any way this trap
Is quite hard
To leave
Maybe because
So sweet

As the memory of you and me
It's so easy to drown in the past
And forget the whole life

And why not?
If there is no chance for a real us
And there is no sense
Because we won't change us

Or the past
And there is not only us
Who we have to care about

I know that
darling
oh go away
please go away from my dreams
I can't stand this
There is too much for us
To manage

And you
Do not want this
Just why you left again
This little door for me open?
Don't you know
I'll look for you through them

Why don't you let me go away for good
If you don't love me enough
To act to care?

You even stop your talk
So what is left?

Oh yes this silly show
of mine
This drama on my site
This comedy too
This me here
For you

Who can't stop writing
Like a mad

Fuck!

At least

Well it is good to know
That you still wish to keep in the touch
Even if it is only me who talks

You must have some fun with me
At least

I admit

and actually
I agree

I can't explain why
really

By the way

It seems we both know this my dear
That this love is nothing but creation of my hungry heart
And it can't live anywhere except this site
That's why this trap is so fine and special

And sweet to live in
Because it is only another dream
Yet so real

Back to your life

Well all that was good
Is gone somehow
Another bitter end
Of this sweet story of us
Maybe it's better like this
Maybe it's better for both

back to your life

We will find new charms soon
I am sure

It will take some time
Of course

But it is just how it works
This loss
Maybe it's better to leave now
When it hurts the most
But will survive
Inside as it was
Just a moment ago

Who knows?

For now we have a story
That's all
And memories too
What to wish more?
Nothing is left I suppose

So leave it up
And back to our life
It's ok too and it is full of new surprises too
I am sure

Touch and go

Yes baby go
Find for yourself
Some more discreet lover than me
I can write my book of life
Without you here

It's more real than you have ever been to me

Thanks for these few moments in space
Thanks for all the poems too
It will stay something for us
This way

And it is ok

Nothing compares

Do you think it is possible to drown for good
In this sadness after you?

There is so many questions still in me
And nothing more I can do

So it will be forever like this?
This madness this dream?

I can play those pictures
Putting thoughts again to the site
Like they were fresh
Like all this still goes on

But it is not true
It's only me here
Talking to the ghost

Not for me

Yes I was willing to give it another try
It's true
Yet not this way, not like this
I don't need the man
Who doesn't trust me enough
To speak
I don't need a coward
And the man who treats me as air
Each time when it is just a little bit
More complicated than it should be
And who lies intensively enough
To be lost himself in it

Yes sometimes it is sweet indeed
Yet after a moment it touches
Just too often, just too much

It's charming sometimes
These dreams
But well
Not like this
You did
To let me know again
How little you care

It is the perfect time to leave
It's not the way
For me to follow any more
Even when you are kind of sweet
In it indeed
Still

Yet not for me
Anymore
Not for me
You live
But do not worry you are safe
I am not femme fatal for you
You are free on your way

There is no consequence of this romance
Except this lost chance

Lost again

The city is calling
Nights still open before
And you strangers
Sing your songs

Like you know
What I want

Of course I am lying

And who will lie to me
So sweetly as you did?
I'll wait for a man like you
Or I'll dream and learn how to lie too
To let them feel good

What else I can do?

Next level

With some of you
I don't need to talk any more
We know enough
Now I just wish you
To do it

We don't need more
Just this

One of the important questions

Are you still curious of me?

Internet

What it is if not
Huge open beautiful
Playground
For all of us to enjoy?

It's a special world
Where we are able to live and play
Together
Fulfilling minds and souls
By something so exciting so good
At the same time we can touch each other too
And gain and lose so much
In one moment in space in one night or day
All your world can be changed

By a single word

That gives you a power to enjoy this world
Or lack of hope

Beautiful dangerous world
Be careful
And enjoy!

Just as much as you can just as much as you want
It's free and it lives inside
And it's so big just as your imagination is
Go follow your dreams and needs
You can have all that you wish here
Believe me

I am here for years with few of my friends
And I'll never leave
It is all just too sweet and too free
To find something else

Here you have your own mind and soul
Shared with these who you like or love
What else to is needed?

Well some other life still
But here is more
So you can play just as you wish
It is amazing, really it is
As much as this love
Which suddenly became eternal in words
I am playing with a time again
Like you were here still with me
And it seems so real

So it is all just an art we can be sure of
It is only mind which creates all
And heart of course

I wonder if a new story begins soon
Or maybe I can live only with you here
You exist in my mind or for real
Doesn't matter now

As long as I still smile
To these words
I had for you
In some moment in space
When we caught our souls
And fell in love

Satisfaction after time

I know that sometimes at night
When you hold her and whisper to her ears
Some sweet things
Both trying to get aroused
You think of me

Yes I know how it feels
And that it is good
We all need such thoughts
Of those who are not present any more
We all need such dreams
At times
When our way is not so clear
And yours is not

I know it
Because I am lost the same
In this dream
We were in

There is nothing wrong in dreams
I think I like to be like this
At least
It is just another form of existence
And it is nice to live
Still

Hello my fellow

I really like to visit your home poet
It seems we live with the same madness in mind
My fellow you are
It's nice I see you are not ashamed of this
Just as me
So we can drink our cup of tea
With my honey and your crème in it
And laugh from this dream
We have here
To survive
Another day
Another love
Which is not enough
To stop
This transmission of mad heart
We both have
It is just this another side of us right?
This a bit more wild more free than we show outside
Yet still the best one we have
By the way I don't know any drug more dangerous
Than this poetry, than yours or my words
Real, sweet madness to drown for good
Who cares by the way?
If we live here or we are not
It is also fun in it
It is also great
Any way
Nice to see you are writing a lot still
I am your reader every day
And I can't stop
I love your mind
Just as I love my own dreams
It is a compliment I think
I'll miss you if one day you disappear
From here

Yes I will

You are one of the best daily things
I have still

This what really hurts

Any madness of your heart
Any wild fantasy
Any lover from your dreams
Present or a lost one

Never hurts so much
As the pain of your child
Crying because something is wrong suddenly
Something happened to his ear

And I don't know how to help him

Good that such moments come and go
And I can go back to the rest
Of my world
To you
And to all other dreams as well

But do not understand me wrong
I am too old to enjoy dreams by my own
They are more wishes of mine now
Something to share with the special one
Something to go for and to enjoy more
Each moment that comes for real
Not only dreams I have here

How to stay young

You just count the time
From one to another event
That matters to you
Everything between
Does not exist
So you saved some of it

A thousand years

The time was never important
For us
And never will be
We are above this
In our dream of eternal love
That can't be crashed
By any little thing
Of our humble existence or weakness
In just one of all possible worlds
We chose to stay for a while

Immortal beloved

I wish to die in your arms
Can you promise me this
My sweet?

Hard to say

Did I break your heart again
For good perhaps
Or did I make you laugh?

I hope this second more

Yet you have been gone
So I am not sure how bad I am for you

Gypsy's wife

My dear man
I wonder if one day
After another age flows
You just stand on the scene
To sing the song
For me

I'll be back hearing your voice
I'll be back
Of course

Because
Each way has its beginning
and the end we both see the one

You and I in song

Remember?

So I'll be back hearing your voice
I'll be back
Of course

Groovy kind of love

I love when you said last time:

"You don't have to be polite Anna
I love you"
You know that either you...
And you are not
We are just as we are
You hidden at times
Me open wide

Each has its ups and downs
I know honey I know
This even too much
At times

But it is fine
It is this mystery on the way that leads us
This is all the fun in it
Isn't it?

Oh darling it all seems ok as long as I feel love in the air
But what if this all disappears one day?

What will stay?
The memory of glorious ancient times

So is it worth it, does it have value
Yes, yes

To jump now
Into the life
Just as we can just as we want
and smile and cry feeling all this again and again
Because there is still nothing else

Worth a while more
I suppose...

Except one thing...

But you are not here

Love...

Is sometimes a simple joy from little signs I can see
And faith that you still live there for me

To one of wolves

Sometimes when you come here
I see
You just check if this is the right moment for you
And after few words you know

It is not
yet

So you go away
To check again
After year
Your meal

This little book to fulfill

I wonder if this is what I do
Makes you feel more horny
Or rather sick though

But I don't care
It's just my way to go
You have nothing to do with this
For now

Even if you still live
here

Somehow

I know it seems that I am a bit cruel for you
Maybe it's just because

You already know

all

Decision

I'm not speaking
With men
Who are not on the same level of naughtiness
As I am

The Common Sense
I have enough at work and at home

Here is free space
For something else
Something more
I guess

So go away from me
All reasonable and good men!

You just spoil the atmosphere
Of my dream land!

All the rest
Who know the rules and the time when they should be broken
And who know what I mean

Come in
Please

And feel at home
Still

A master of love

You give nothing
But it feels like it's everything
You can live for

You take away nothing
But it feels like it's everything
What was worth to live for

Winter time

It is the best time
For the suicide
If you plan this final act
You can simply go outside
Walk some time
Then rest in a forest
Looking at the stars
Saying your last hello and last good bye
To this special beautiful life
You have had

and die

A kind of beauty too isn't it?
Well yes indeed nice end

Yet it's still something to do here
So there is no point to go
I'll stay in bed instead
Until I have some

So no goodbye from my side
Until there is still something to dream about
Something to follow too
Something to do
and to enjoy
but it's nice to know
that you always have
some opportunity
and some choice

Empty spaces

So it was me
Who killed this love
Finally

Now it's time for a little dance
In the dark

And for this feeling of being invisible
again

Yes it was best like this
After death there will be another life instead

Just as you said

Coming back to life

Indeed at the end
There is always you
Who know yourself the best
So only you can understand why
Some actions were done
Some promises broken
Some feelings killed

Yes it is you who know all the story
Of your bright and dark soul
It is you
Who has to fight every day
With your own games
and try to win at the end
another day

With a little bit of spice in it
To enjoy its taste
The best

The variety

In fact there are only a few things that matter in life
And from now all depends on how you can see and feel them
How you are able to describe, talk, live by it

There are only a few things
But such a huge variety in the way we get them
Indeed there is nothing more - just this
And time to understand or spoil things

Yes I did this

I killed my love
It was me who did this
Piece by piece
Using words
Using pictures too
And these actions...
Being honest like a death
With you
I did this
Why?
Maybe it was just too hard
To stand so much happiness
At times
Maybe because
I am bad enough
To do so
Maybe because we had too much time between
Too much space
I don't really know why
It happened
But I can't change this now
I went too far
And I am going still
To fulfill any silly dream
Which comes suddenly
Where could I go now
If not ahead?
Well, I can just stop, I know
But then...
Then it will be the same
Do you think I am proud of this?
No I am not
I regret
And I won't forget you
Any sweet moment we have had too
Darling
But I have to live still
With or without you here..

hey you

I don't think so I have been changed so much
It's just that you can't look at me any more
with love in your heart

and I understand

I know it's mostly my fault...

I am sorry

I was not strong enough

To keep this stone

It's about

It's not all about just taking and giving
It is about a feeling of primary joy and openness
It is all about being free and safe
On the way to each other on the way to an adventure
That the future of both of you seems to be every day
Like it was still just the beginning

Hard choice

I can't decide yet
If I'd prefer to be your Mistress or your slave
Both sides of the drama seems exciting the same
So it's hard to say

Your Girl in a Photo

I was in love with you
From the first poem I read from you

Little smile to my own world

It's so easy to be the Queen
In my home made
United Kingdom

A woman needs her soul

And you shouldn't stop believing
That it's you who hold the key
And also you shouldn't forget
That smile is just a smile
and kiss is just a kiss

Nothing else

It all doesn't matter now my sweet
I have you forever
Inside me

You want me or you are away
It is all here

Gone but still inside me

Do you think it is the end when you have gone ?
You are wrong
I can now even feel you more
You became my every thought
Dream and joy
You became sweet memory of my own
Bitter too
I know you like to be like this
It's more tasty, more real
I know you my broad minded and down to earth man
And now even when you had to go away
I still own you like a dream I wish to stay forever in
I know how to keep you still
And I don't ever wish to cure myself
It'd be like a cutting half of me
This more beautiful, more mad and deep
I won't do this
I'll drown with this ship
Instead

Dance me to the end of love

I am always the same
And I back to places I love the most
It's just how it is
And how it should be
The way is always the same
As you know well
We don't need to hurry up
to the end
We can dance still
Or I can
Your choice
I'm here

Always inside my own madness and dream
I'm not going anywhere

So you can do
If you enjoy

Come and dance me
To the end of love

A perfect man for me

It has to be a boy still
Naughty, free
But always good and gentle for me
Even being harsh at times when it's needed or sexy... depends
But he knows when he can
The man who never pushes me to do things I'd not wish to do my self first
But who let me wish all these things to do...

Yes perfect man
Who is you
It's good to meet
At last

and keep or lost
Doesn't really matter
It's just a matter of time and place and life as you can say
But this what you have because of him
Stay forever
In your soul
Like a crack like a goal
Just to keep just to dream about
And dance inside your soul
Just like this to go on

Sweet temptation

Another sweet temptation
Is growing inside my world
It's you my wolf

You delightful man
Who comes to me
Each time I call my love
Dancing on my burning fields
After another war
We just had a moment ago

You who support me when I am weak and alone
You who watch my dance when I got strong
You who could be my love
As well
Yet for now
My soul-mate
I adore your presence here
You know
And I appreciate
This hope
For more

Sensitive

As less you touch her, press her
Then more she can feel you and need you

After time silence is the best language of love

She needs this calm space
After storm

Just nothing and still so much

In fact darling man of mine
We didn't really build
Anything so far
That we would fight for
We don't have any child nor home

And I know that I should just move on
Stop all these dreams

And just live
As before

Like you were not here
At all

Just why it's not that simple?
Why this lives its own life in me
Like all was real?

Being on one of these sides

One is sure
I am not a puritan's soul

Why for?

Just don't understand this pride
Of being so accurate and mean
In everything

When you can enjoy more
The taste and the touch and some words
Whatever you can see or find beautiful around

To taste to try it all

Why not?

About importance

You are as important as much as you are willing or able to give from yourself
To this world or the person you are important to.

Just watching you still

I think there is nothing but poetry
In your life
But this is a main reason I love to come back to you
and watch
Even not touching you
Nor saying a word
Even not being your woman, love or whore

I am just coming here
and drink your mind
Like it was my story and like you were mine

Nothing new

You just compare:
Sensitivity
Believes
Dreams
Chemistry

Then you go for it

You feel this mixture of smiles and tears
And you know
That's it

Nothing new
Indeed

Yet so sweet

It's gone

So you don't know my thoughts
It's cut this line between
Any naughty fantasies any dreams or sorrows
This mind became closed to you

I don't even know if I miss this so much
I enjoy being with myself right now
Sharing just a part of the story
At times

Yes maybe it's better like this
Me is just me
There is no need to share all these
Little secrets

So you don't know about a man I was thinking about
Going by bus recently
He reminds some old friend of mine
Or lover
Yes I was thinking of him this way too
Just a little thought on a bus
To make journey more pleasant

You always liked to know
Whom I can think about this way...and how

Many times it was you who created another story
Yes sometimes I miss this still

But well
I don't even think to send you any message any more
It's all gone

Comfortable place to stay

I think you always knew
That this what is called "a real world"
Is not really interesting to me
Yes a fiction seems much more comfortable
To live in

Sometimes it is even hard to find
This thin line between
The two of it

Yet still I prefer to live here
Hard to say why
More colourful
More free?
Wild?

Any way when you grow up
All seems a bit boring
Isn't it?

I still wish to laugh at times
That's why

A thing about treasures

I like to find my treasures by myself
When someone try to push me
To buy them
I don't like them anymore

The beautiful thing for me has to be find by me
Then it pleases
And it is special and sweet

Nice common truths

Nice simple truths just heard recently
In a few of these lovely films
One: You are this that you love not this that loves you
Second: 2 things are important in life - to find your love and to live each day as it was the last one
I think I can agree with this
Yes good beliefs

Who knows the best way for you and me

I still have a feeling
That I had you just as much
As I was able to take myself
As I was strong enough to call and wish you
As I was able to act to touch you

and I could go for more
If I knew better way for it, perhaps
or if I was just less greedy
Who knows?

But well sometimes
There is only moment we can really enjoy
So it was like this with you and me
Possibly you never planned offer even this
So maybe it's good that I also act not only dream

I know that you only love me when I love you
Completely, for good unconditionally
And even then I can't be sure
If we ever meet again

These are your rules in the story
But I always go my own way

So what else to tell
I just hope you are ok

Yes so it was just another dream

So it seems
That you can live
Without me

It is just somehow sad
That we end up
Before it really start

Even after all these years
I have this feeling
That it was just the beginning
Of our real dance

But yes it was just a dream
Before the computer screen
and still is
here

Missed with myself

Some says that we can feel not enough life
or too much
It is an art to feel we have it
Just enough
Yet maybe it's good to feel this way at the end
As for now it's good to be a bit hungry I think
Just why at times
I'm still like at the beginning
Or I didn't even start anything yet

It makes me feel not so good
Like all I have done so far was not exactly this
What I wish

Just where to go now
Where to go
And what for?

Little sweet touch

It's hard when suddenly you feel and touch
Exactly this that you want and then it's gone
And you know that all you can have from now
Is just this sweet memory and little hope
That one day maybe you can feel this again
And come for more

Golden words

Two Gold maxima of our love:
"I don't trust you because I know you"

And whatever we do together and no matter how far we go through this you can always say:
"I haven't done anything that you didn't ask for"

And it's true you perfectly know me and this that I want you to do to me
You perfectly know how to make me feel good being beside you
That's why I want you

Love and death

You are only one man who's hand I could die from and still keep smiling
Love is so close to death

You can feel happy to die when it is needed
as you can feel death in you when it is gone
This love

Amazing it is
And so full of surprises

There is still something to live for
and enjoy
Like your breath inside my mouth and the taste of your tongue
or the way you touch me telling me what you want to do to me
and how gentle you are with this and brutal too
Just amazing how you make me feel so good, so yours

I have never met anything anyone more delicious on my way
Than you

So far...

Matter of love

It seems that there is so many definitions of love
As people involved
And so many of them seems so wrong
So what?
It's still this thing that we are looking for
No matter how strong we pretend that we don't
No matter how many times we try and we are broken
Love still flows
As a river of light
Through our life

We can't stop it no matter how much we try
We don't even know where it leads us
To the end or to another wonder land

About a death and hope

Death - just the end of this play
But don't worry if your faith is strong
And you are good you have a chance
To go to the second level

Some nights I can feel you there

Some nights I can feel you are there wolf
I am just not ready yet
To come

My head is too busy
and my thoughts still belong to another man

Yet each time we meet
I am happy you are here
Waiting and leaving your footprints
In my longing town

One day our time can come
For now only these few smiles that we always feel
Can save us close to each other

I know you want more
That's why I can't come
Yet

More of this sharing

I know it is selfish
But it's such a difference
When it is me who share some of these sweet details
With someone like you who I know wish to be close
And who enjoys each moment of intimacy
We can feel together sharing whatever

And it all turns in smiles
or even excitement at times

and we just know
what it is all about

building another story
even without any intention
it just comes whenever we meet
That's it

Our little silent talking game

Yes I enjoy to listen your silence
Just forgive me if sometimes
I can be wrong with interpretation

You know it's everything about the feeling and imagination
And this can leads to unknown or to being a fool!
Even in such a familiar topic
As my own and your soul
In this little play
We go on
Somehow

Waiting still

This what you gave me
Is all this free space
For dreams

and from this time
All depends from how deep and wide
I can jump, swim, see and feel
Whatever I wish

And you are somewhere here
Waiting still

Behave as you came first here

Yes making mistakes is a human thing
The point is to know or to learn
When and how
Turn around

To stay on your way
This right one
With enjoyment and song and dance
Inside

Just to make few more footprints
In this book of life
Making it more precious more wide or funny too
Before we leave
For good

Love will tear us apart

It's amazing at times
How little you know about this war
That goes on so long
Between us

You are still so unaware
It makes me feel sorrow for you
And for me
Of being still here
Like there is no way out
But it is
It's just we didn't notice yet
This right moment

Or we are waiting
For something to come
But it won't

These are only silent battles
That you don't recognize
Until I say
That I wish to go away

Then you can see I am a bit mad
You wish me to change
And I say it's hard
Or I am not able to do that
And I am selfish and I am bad
And you are right

And we are still here
Isolated closed
In two separate worlds
Like nothing happen
From one to another wave
Of sorrows
But there is a war
That you don't know about

Don't worry you won't die here
The only thing you can lose or win
Is me

The story of life

Well in fact
it's nothing but the story of meetings, leavings and their
consequences

Evolution

Life is an evolution
But you missed my direction
So it seems I go alone
In to the unknown

About love again

Yes it must be true
Love is just a magical, fragile, intimate
experience of your own soul
It's good if you have possibility to express this somehow
To share with this one
Yet you must be careful
Too much love can be hard to stand
I suppose
So just dance in your heart
And learn how to not scare away
This someone you care
This delicate sound is the best to gain
Not too loud not too much
Just dance inside first
Enjoy or suffer and play within
With this feeling that comes so rare so sweet
Sometimes stay silent too
If it works good

It is a fragile thing
This love
More waiting in this than fight
It comes naturally
In sounds, touches and kind of wisdom

Don't make too much noise
Just listen its voice
And never use force
Rather a beautiful song
To let her know
That you love

I wish we could do something still

My darling man
Before we leave this world
I wish we could do something beautiful
Together
It can be a book, a song or our home
Whatever
Because as we both know
We are only guests on this world
And our journey is in the middle of the way
If we have a chance
So still so much and so little time left
To put our footprints our little bricks
On the wall
Until we say our final goodbye

But before we start
To do this something great
We can meet at least
For a cup of tea or a drink
What do you think?

Summer wine

Another summer came
And you are still
so sexy man
Who can have every woman
Of this world
If you only want

Just what for?
If it's hard to keep
Even this one
Me...

Anyway it's all fun
Nothing more
So enjoy the summer

My beloved

My Grand book of wishes

First of all
I wish you to follow my thoughts
Even these silly, boring, repeating ones
With these all errors I do
And that you try to understand them all
I know it is all mad at times
Touching too and it makes you feel
Bad or good
But you have to look

You have to look at me
Without it it's nothing here

And love is just the word
Without the real background

And I wish it was true
This all you
Not only the moment in space
For naive silly whore
Who is looking for something
She should not
No this I don't want

I wish a few things more
But this I wrote before
So you know
And I wish this one night too
With you
And that you massage my feet
Being again so caring and sweet
Telling me all I want and need to hear
Making me yours for good
Yes this I wish the most
And that all you say was true
And that I was able to catch this somehow
and never lose
And I wish to be more sure
Of tomorrow
With you

I know it is too much...

You better hide

I think that ready scenarios are not good to me
I do not enjoy to act in them like this
I like unexpected things to feel
that comes suddenly
so you never know
what it can be
I am sorry

Differences between some women and men

Some men try to get so many women as they can
Some women try to not have so many men
as many try to get them

It seems like all the rest don't have so much to do
In this field so they have some rest
All can change in time
But the rule seems general
Though not for all

Anyway it's a bit funny
And let's run or run away or rest
Depends from time and place and needs
Yet still we keep this play
Or observe
To really live

It's not a point

In love
There is not a point
To be always so perfectly honest and true
To each other

More it's to feel comfortable being as you are
And still feel safe that whatever it can be
All will be fine
And you are still the right one
And dear
For him

And the same from another side

Of course
That's how it works

My sweet thing

Is this life not just a moment in space?
So just take my hand and let's walk together
as we enjoy each other right now so well
No names nor place are important for this
So let's just be here or there and dream and smile
And make that we love to make
Some special beauty in space, music, dreams, love

My sweet thing you are for me
My treasure to enjoy a day
So let's stay and see
What this brings

Is it a rain or a ray of the sun
Is it a thought, a touch or a dream
We just live by
doesn't matter
We were born to be here and to meet
Let's enjoy it

No words needed

Somehow words don't flow anymore
It seems like I've said everything to you
There is no need for more
Repeating could destroy
The meaning
of us

So now only a play of thoughts
Inside my head
Let me dance
Still for you

So I do

No call

Yes I'm quite silent recently I know
But whatever comes to my mind to share with you
Seems so cheap, too sentimental and piteous
So I prefer to stay calm by my own
Maybe I could live without you maybe I could
It was nothing but words
And all was already said before
So it's time to stop

No call, no wish, no hope
For more

Only waiting for another day
That will come

With or without
Love

Any way it was always just a dream
That you are here
With me

We become a bit cruel with time

We are getting to be a bit cruel
With time
Have you noticed?

Keeping these little sorrows
Years by years
We do not even know
When it starts

You have to be ready
To face this now

On this stage of life
We are

After all we went through
Together
You should be aware

What I can do to you
When I feel not enough

Love

Sinners and honest men

Sinners and honest men
Will never understand each other

So better if they stay away
And play different games

They are not friends

About some wonderful things

You know what is wonderful between us Darling?
That whatever we do
Even being hard at times, bad, impossible, wrong
Or not being at all for long
Still whenever I see you
I can feel like this adventure just began
and it's so exciting and so good
To be near you
And this mix of smiles and tears inside
And this comfortable confidence
That I am beautiful for you
Yes it is sure
In your smiles it is
And in the way you kiss
I can't explain this well
But it's just
That anything else
Doesn't really matter and doesn't compare
And we can do or say whatever
It'd change nothing at all
Smiles and tears will go on

Aspiration

What is your favorite aspiration?

I'd like that someone find the hidden beauty
In me
Then make a piece of art from it
And invited me to the process
Of Creation
And... we could both just disappear
After all

Silence and sounds

Sometimes it's like a sea of silence
You have to get through
Waiting for noises
You long to make
In the darkness
One more time

Sweet secrets

There is so delightful sweetness
In some hidden secrets
If you know how to keep them
Alive
And to feed yourself
By this violent kind of pleasure
You can taste in them
When they become
The most valuable and mysterious
Part of your life.

Then there is no return
From this deeper kind of world
You live by
Or you live because

Until death
or
Until they become
Ready to be shared
With all
But be aware
They can lose its natural charm
Or they can transform
To some new form

But do not hurry up with this
You never know
So
For now

Just enjoy
And keep them still
As deep as you need

They are
To make your days and your life

So SPECIAL

Little warning

This what I don't like much
Except obvious things:
Real violence, wars etc
In this what you can call
Everyday life
Of common guy
Well so this what I don't really like much
Is too many questions and advices

Yes I think such things annoys me the most
and the boring talk of course
I am sorry to say so..
Everything else
Is acceptable

Even if it is simple or complicated
and brings some unsuspecting things
In to your soul
Or hurts your feelings or ego

We need free space
To make steps
Even wrong
So don't ask too much
and don't say you know
If you wish to stay close

Hidden sky

In the framework of your hidden love
I can feel freedom just enough to fly
And to share the flutter of my wings
With you

I don't need to go away
Because your chains
Are wide enough
Invisible but strong
So I know where I belong
And I wish to be back still
Yet I go my way discovering this world
Like a child
And we both know that this is what I need and I enjoy
So we have this large space and time to play
And this is ok
As long the memory of your sight
Is still alive

A way

Is any other journey for human worth a while
than this deep one in to your heart and mind?

We can travel just on the way to each other
and explore this as much as we can

Walking on the fields cities and deserts seems quite empty thing
If it doesn't let you know more about yourself and about someone else...

Love and too much of it

Sometimes it's a bit hard to decide
What is worst
To not have love at all
Or to have it enough

If it is inside you and you can feel it hits the ground it seems a miracle
But noises of the crowd who don't really know anything - especially you
Seems a bit annoying though

These are days you can't bear even one loving man beside you
and all you long for is just a silence and a distant song of the memory you still keep inside

to survive

Art is everything

Anything you are not able to turn in art
Is nothing special

And it doesn't really matter what the word "art" means to you

It's everything
You can live for

You here

And who exactly you wish to be here?

A single man to date with
The lover or the killer of me?

It's your choice
It's only a dream

so feel free

Poetry and you

I let you in
and
Nothing really happened
What a disappointment...

By the way what actually this poetry is?

It's me of course can be you and he, she, whoever

The voice I am never able to speak
With people
But it is growing in me
So it has to be said

Then I write

It has to be said
Because it is the only real sign of this
in fact quite humble existence I have

That is worth a while, a smile, a life...for me

Not even all the time
But you can always chose
What you like the most

It has to be said
Because it is the one thing

Real and Alive

Inside

A question...

What form of me you wish to have now my dear?
How to love you still
When all seems so distant again
suddenly somehow
Far away

but always
I do and you too

so come whenever you need

my love

Diagnosis

Can you tell me
What is so wrong with your marriage already?
Well I can say
It's the peculiar lack of intimacy
It's the fear to ask basic questions or to answer them
It is the lack of ability to share important thoughts
That should unite
But they only takes us apart
Unseen
Unsaid
Not realized
The silence
and the lack of cooperation
on a deeper level of existence
Can we survive?

I am afraid it's too late
My darling

I found out myself
With someone else

I didn't know I can be so cruel...
you are so delicate so good
and I am so bad
It's at times hard to stand...
and that I am such a closed book for you
all this time

It is a real drama in fact
I just hit you to death

and you didn't notice...

Maybe it's better like that
It's because you live outside
and you don't see clear
so we can live in peace still...

and I can stay here like a fool in space
Until you find this page
and feel what I had to say once upon a time
and you will drown in this sea I've build here...

but for now
sleep well my dear
it's not a time for any war yet
so

Happy New Year

And what is the truth?

It is not a matter of this truth at all
There is plenty of them as many points of view

This that matter is the point of your view and the way you go

And what this gives to you
Means for you

and don't be too serious
it's not worth it

so enjoy, enjoy the night

and another New Year

Humble words

these are moments when you can feel
that even simple write can be just a part
of your own decay and you still go on

even when you know it is wrong
but in fact the strength of this act
is visible for you only

and you can't stop it now
because it's just the middle of the way

in your circle of life

Coincidence

Darling
It's so good that
When I'm going in to madness
Step by step

You in mean time learn
How to be a doctor

So when I'll be in your hands
You will cure me

But

Do you really want me

Better stay away

I think I shouldn't be with you
I shouldn't even think of you

I am too jealous
So obsessively jealous
of anyone who comes closer to you
even in few words or in my imaginary

It's sick
I know it..

I never felt this way about anyone
so far
and I come closer too
to one or few

I have to stay away
simply stay away

and wait
just

for what?

Me and write

What are you doing there at night?
I set free demons into the sky
So they can enjoy a little freedom
Are you all right?
Yes all fine

This is a secret place

Please don't look at these words
With the thin heart
Wrapped in the tight frame of conventions and rules
It's not a place here for moral support
This is the secret place
That we all have in dreams
So better look deeply in to the mirror
Of your soul
And see what it is longing for
Before you say what you think
Of me...
Please

This mortal coil

If at times I do not play soft enough with you
Forgive me
It's because
I am always aching without the sight of you
No longer sure of anything
Then thoughts go mad
Playing their battles defending, hitting you
for my own uncertainty
I feel because you are no longer here

So little I have you
And so much I feel you I see you inside my head

It never change
See my darling, so many years and it's still like we just have met
And it was the beginning of the story
Each day each year the same
Yet so different
But today I learn one more time
How to take a pleasure from this silent signs
You give
To let me know you are here still
For me

The night is over

I'm so happy you came again
Lover
You recognize well
My call in the dark
Then you are
My wolf

Turning tears in to smiles
Just like that
By one snap
So easily you do that
and the night is over

The spy

Do you feel me
On the other side of this screen
So much as I feel you?
Whenever you come closer here and make a single step
I see it
I am the spy in our house of love
I can't help
I see all you do
I almost feel your breath and your thoughts
and I share
I share
as much as I can
until I feel you are so close
and dreams grow up fast in mind
and maybe you hear my thoughts for a while..
and you enjoy
and I wish
I wish
you could stay here
for me
longer
a bit
just a bit
until another dream
I can share
and I can live by
comes
because
you are here
again

for me
so close

The tree of dreams

A hundred dreams
Come inside
Whenever you touch me
By your beautiful mind

Don't stop
please

go on
and stay here
near

so I can feel them
and live enjoying their melody and smell
so easy to touch they are now

like you were here
beside
inside
me
still
I love it
and I always will

Love and poems

I love that
Writing another poem for you
is a bit like making love
With the same man from years
and still with the same flame
it comes each day each night each year...

It's an art and love in one
So perfect bound so fine

and

I love that
I can still
Enjoy this one single favorite topic in me
I have it from the time we've met

At times I am just not sure
How much you enjoy
this open love

yes I know this writing on this site
Is like showing me naked one more time
before all who comes to watch us...

but you love a bit naughty things too
so you can enjoy I am sure you do

and I love that I can be mad with you as much as I want
It's quite comfortable

Bad boy

How bad I have to be today
To be exciting for you
My bad boy?

Hard to say all is born in a moment you come
But everybody knows

That being just nice
Is not enough

For this juicy colourful life we go through
to gain new smiles
together

The best that you do

The best thing in this that you do
Is the way you make me feel beautiful enough
To wish to seduce you
and this is all I long for
to be like this to you

seductive and beautiful

Dreams come and go

So you worry of anything that could ruin
This relationship we have
It's good to know you care of this
Though we have a bit different points of view
for the real danger we can face on the way
I am afraid...

but we both want to keep this alive
and this is good
I shouldn't worry too much
before the time
and just enjoy your presence
in my world
that's all

dreams come when you come closer
but they all die in a moment you are not here
I am not enough selfish, greedy and cruel too
to run for them alone

and I know that for you
it'd be a nightmare if I do

so the only place for you and me
is here
I know darling, I know my sweet
so don't worry

and dream still
No one ever will know
about you and me
except this place here

but it's only a play garden of my own desires and dreams
so not a big deal

Tomorrow

It's amazing how easily you make me so hungry so greedy
and one day seems again like an ocean of longing
to have you again the way I need
just for me

Just a spark of your sight

So this is the end for now...
Not a day but maybe a month or a year
of waiting
I was too intense perhaps
So now it's time to calm down

You have gone
Nothing to share
Nothing to live by inside

Just a memory of the spark
and hope

that you will be back

I am not creative

No my darling man
I am not creative
I just need to tell my story
When something special begins
and it all starts with you
Each time you come
My beautiful open book
My adventure with no other end
Just with you
In your arms again
Cuddled

It's you this sweet raise the roof of my head
I love to have
To move, to scream, to wait
and to show
what I find so beautiful
in this life in this world...

Don't you know?

Nightingale

Come lover sacrifice my land
So I could enjoy any stone we pass across
Any house we kissed each other beneath
Any grass we lie down to rest
Any path we walked through holding each other

Any piece of the ground and the air we breathe
To remember and to comeback
With a secret embrace to these places

For now they are all useless
No meaningful enough
To enjoy to remember
To notice they exist at all

So come soon
I am calling you
The way I can
The way I find
Tempting enough
By nightingale I got today
For you

Please come

My love

In life

In life
there is time of fuck
and there is time
of poetry
less interested of this make wars
or other bad things
besides we are all just a voyeurs
of other people life and fantasies

of course in mean time there is plenty other things we do like hard work for living and some daily stuff like making our beautiful children growing up if we have some, keeping family and friends in good or bad mood, but it's nothing what I am talking about right now

this what I mean is us and basic forces that lead us to act

love and hate
and space between
one or another feeling that let us move
in this world

right or wrong

basic things but natural...

I don't know where this smile came from suddenly
in me...
must be again some sweet memory...

A balance

At times I am a bit confused
Of how much lies we need to spread around
To keep all close to us happy enough...

It's also an art to know this
balance between right and wrong weight of illusion...

How it works

You effect me
And then I have something to tell
To this world
About a beauty and about love
About a desire and about a betrayal too
About everything what is real and meaningful
All these hidden secrets of the heart flow unwrapped in to the open space
Who knows what they do when I close this book
I don't care too much

Sometimes I feel like someone who after a thousand years of silence
suddenly needs to speak

So forgive me
If it is too much to handle
Too much to keep

I don't know the end my self yet...
I create and share to live

But don't worry about my home
In mean time all is going on

Another meal is prepared, another day fulfilled
By also sweet little things I share with them
They just ask at times: mom
Why you talk to yourself all the time?
and what do you say?

Oh nothing my babies it's just another life
I have inside nothing to worry about
It's just my another world to live by

Finish your dinner now

And you the man who is still beside me
You know that all this what I keep here
Is just an illusion of my mad mind perhaps
You believe that, don't you?

Anyway you look great and I hope that in some way
You are still happy to meet me
Even if I am not ordinary wife to you
But you never cared of things like this as I know...
You knew I am still kind of girl and that's all
Just a fun and a specific type of trip
We decided to start and to keep
Until it is working well for you and me
How long then?
Can you say, can you see?

Oh better to not think of the future now
We are as we are and we live as we live so far
Where it leads?
I don't know

I am on the way to unknown
Dreams are dreams
But now is now
The only one real thing
We grab in hand

and this another space another life inside

I am just greedy as always I...
Forgive me and you too
That I have you all
Maybe I shouldn't, who knows?

Wolf and me

Oh I didn't know there is more beautiful wolves
In this world
What a sweet surprise
Yes you bring me smiles
Sir
And you amazed me last night
The beauty and power of your sight
And yes I am a bit shy
In my daily life
at times..
If you wanna know
But not when I meet the man
and the wolf
Then I am not
Then I know how to speak
and how to wait too
and how to enjoy
All

Piss of

There is so many things you should simply enjoy
but you don't
anymore
You are so piss off with all
and wish to send everybody to hell
including yourself
good that after all you back to your senses again
and it's still like nothing happened

Rainy days

It's amazing how every day is different
and how much uncertainty I can still find inside
about you and me, the future or even this moment we live
I feel like this boat I am on and I can't go out is sinking
And I am the main responsible for it
but maybe it was always only me
who was going to drown in all this

They just came here to save me
and I should be strong now
to keep going on this at least as long as they need
There is still not the right time for change
I know
So why this mess inside, why this fight for?
I really don't know

You achieved precisely nothing in fact to do that
Just go on the way you start
There is no way out
So keep smiling and enjoy
That's why you are here
for the sake of god!

And you darling I know you will be back too
We need each other
In some magical way we do
and we live together
Even just in mind and it's fine
You sweet little dream of mine

Don't worry baby I will be fine
It's just at times
This black cloud doesn't let me see things clear enough
but after a rain there is always a sun
so it doesn't matter

It's all right too
if you can't come now or soon
I've learnt to wait
For this what I wish
and in this waiting is also some charm
My sweet full of life man
from the green wonderland
I found out once upon a time

The light

So you've been back to turn the light in my world
How beautiful
The witch is gone sweetness came back to my lips and words
And all around can breathe again
With me at home
of course we need our dreams to live
they are part of us
just as you are part of me
and when you disappear
I do not exist
Just a shadow of me
Pretends something still
To let them believe
That I am here

House of love

With you
Even a grand serious LOVE with all its hard rules and consequences
Seems attractive and not scaring at all
and this lack of freedom at our home
you announce
Is like an open gate to the unknown world of wonders so wide
That I never felt outside
It's like enter to real story I was only read about
So far...

Empty house

There is not love here anymore
So don't come

"It's Beyond My Control!"

You have had to be really bored of me
So it's you who ruin all in once
With such an ease
I never had so much force in me
To do it
But you know after years
It's not such a tragedy
As it was before
It was not even so hard to delete you from my list
And from my world
That you hate so much right now
Suddenly
Good bye love of my life
I hope you will enjoy
This what you have there
And what you have done
I failed and it seems I am not worth to enter this house
We never really build we never really had
An idle stupid dream
This you and me
Indeed

Not the end

You knew it couldn't end up like this
didn't you?
My jealous man

Surrender at discretion

It doesn't matter what was wrong and what even could be
I promise to be a good girl
and I will be
you know you are a necessary and the basic component of my dream
you can't disappear
and I can't go away too
it' just without any sense to do
you stay and me too
and we work for new smiles still
I hope I won't make you feel bad again
My dear man
and I understand now
that you have had right
to be so mad
it's you who can chose
the right dream for both not me
until you live here

They are mine

These words I long to hear from you
Every day
But I know you can't repeat them too often
So they remain
Powerful and fresh
Each time
They come back with you
so I could be sure
more
and to stop mourning
in the time of silence and uncertainty

If you ask

If you want to know what I like
Well I like fishing in the great depth of life
Catching sparks

My fresh breeze

I love the way you are for me
This fresh breeze in the air
You gonna make me smile
Each time I see you here
You make me feel
Young forever with you
A dancing girl
Just as I love to be
My dear boy
My dream
Go on
Please

A difference between the war and you

The topic of war can be interesting for a day
to recognize situation see whose decision I accept less or more than all I can do is to let others decide about the shape of the world and the number of killed or survived

But the topic of you is eternal
I can study you through years and each day seems different and more fascinating and new pictures of us coming to my head and new dreams are born and I can fulfill life by this colourful influence of your spirit to my soul and live by this forever
waiting another touch

Oh what the war than means until it doesn't touch my own life or yours?
Just a bad news

I need to put a spell on you every day new

I have a spells in my head
Those need to spread
Like I want you to be mine
Forever
Like I need you to be here
In any form available
You can be a link in net
A sound of the song you send on your site
A message
A hope for a meeting
A trill of the sight of you
But you have to be near
With me
Always
Because I don't know if I could ever enjoy this world
Without you
So I will spread this song
To keep you with me
Just like this
In my dreams still
Until another day will come
A day for us
and our love
in touch

You touched me virtually

You touched me virtually
One more time my magical boy
You know well how to keep this madness in heart
I wonder how many songs you have still in hand
To make me yours
And so in love with you
Forever
How I love this word
Used for you
Even if some say
It never works this way
I love it
And I wait
For more
Miracles
That comes
From the sound of you
My man,
My ghost of love
The spirit I keep in me
To live

Pain of love

This love seems painful at times yes
I didn't know though how much this beautiful pain I need
To live
Until we've met

Am I able to hurt you?

If the answer is YES
so you are the right one

The importance

Nothing is more important
Than this what can happen
Between us

If it isn't
It means
That nothing really happens
Don't you know?

The slight differences

I am trying to save this all
What you are trying to hide

From some point of view
I can see kind of cooperation between us
In this matter

I will save all this what you will lost
And you will save all other things around

Thank you

Needs
I need to be like an open book
You need to be a secret lover though

And we both respect each other
This way love turned into signs in space
And our minds create magic to live by
Just like a faith
And hope

It is somehow wonderful
And you know that magic is all I can believe in
Especially this one that we can feel

Hidden things and exceptions

Generally I don't like hidden things
At all
Except these few
That I share with you

The temperature of love

Too many words
Too much heart away
It was too much of me by your side today
So it's time to go away

Waiting

One funny thing

There is one funny thing with you
It seems that I always try to force the doors that are always open
But I keep doing it and I am always a bit surprised
Seeing you there with open arms for me and this sexy smile
Yet again I start every day with you from the beginning
My new old dance for you my song
To win your heart like it was still
Not in my hands

Maybe this is how I understand love?

Or maybe I just feel safe with you to do whatever I need or wish to do
Having hope that nothing will change the way you feel with me

Or maybe you just helped me to enjoy myself better and discover things or just being me because
Suddenly I want this all and I need to be like this

You using the right word, the right glance or maybe the right spell
You create the sea of love in me that I need to flood you in and keep you like this naked wet and wishing more
Sometimes it works sometimes I have to wait but I need all this still
It's amazing thing this life with you really!

This way love seems like watching and showing carefully or spontaneously but always with the same interest and need to see and show more

And this is what I love about us
And in you and me
This never ending story

Your album

Hard to say what touch me more
Your pictures with these nice looking women around you
Who you work with or you have fun with I don't really know
Or pictures of your family that you love to put between us
Like a paves before my love
I think I am not doing the same to you
You know I could flow like a river to find new world with you
Searching a way to keep a safe place for all we are with now too
But you are afraid of this I know
It was never me that you really chosen
To be with for real
I am nothing but a little shadow on your soul
Little ghost of love to keep inside
To fulfill empty days with some charm, noise and warm
Yes this is who I am
Not a big deal in fact
Just a song, a poem, a thought, a smile, sometimes tears too
Something that let you feel a little bit more
Even just excitement at times too
Just a moment in space
That's all
Yet still you are everything to me what I want
I can't help that you become my world
And from this time I can't find anything else to enjoy
But it is still touching
All this what you show me now
But I wish to watch and cry
For all that I wish to have but I can't
We all have such things haven't we?
I am not the one like this
It's quite common sin
And I am guilty too
I can't enjoy my days so much
As this longing I have for you
I drowned for good
I can't help, can't explain this too
I just need to watch and feel and have some hope
For this what I want
At least I've found this thing
I have my way inside, my need
To keep you inside me
And in this little wish to see you again
And to feel love in your words and touch
Even if it is so fleeting I need to stay waiting
And watching you, there is nothing else I can do

Please stay and bright my day

I was always searching a light
And then you came in to my life,
How nice,
But now please stay
And help me to fight with all black thoughts that come
From time to time,
Don't be too scared of them
Just stay and speak to me
So they all gone again
And I can smile to you,
My beautiful,
How I am happy that you came
To bright my days
To teach me passion and love
That I never believed can be real
Until we've met and this just happened
My darling

You are the man with the real passion and love in your words
That heats women hearts
At least mine
That is burning each time you stay near
Please never change
And come again here
When you see me walking in the darkness without you again
Or when I'm using my charms for another man
Who could take me away from you
Because I am yours for good
Remember

Smile, smile not

Yes you know how to put smile on my face
But you know as well this how to get it away
It's just I take all too seriously
So it's touching

So silly I am
With this

But how not to be
When I feel
Each word of yours
By all senses
By whole heart
And soul
How?

A Mistake

For a moment I thought
That it is a conversation
But it's again just a talk of mad woman in space
Nothing else
How sad

An alternative

If we can't live together
Maybe we could die together
At least?

The killers – Shadow play

The killer can be a woman who brings your child
The killer can be a man you spent the night with
The killer can be a life you can't bear

Be strong if you wish to stay to the end of the show
If not, well it's just a matter of time
But why worry so much
Enjoy and find this real thing you care about
It has to be something special for you
Another way, what would be worth this entire world?

The answer is always the same and you know it well
So why worry now?
Stay strong and smile to all
That's how it works

It must be love

You make me feel sick too easily
It must be love

I am not a killer baby

Yes I am not a killer baby
But when you treat me too bad
I need to hurt you

And kill you
The way I find attractive
And you perfectly know
What this means

What I am afraid
Is that we will play this way
Again

I wish it was different
You know
But this is you
And this is me

And this is how it is
With us
This game starts

It was your choice
Not mine

But this is you
And this is me
Darling

So

I think you know
What this means

I won't ask you again
This is the end

Good bosses and you

Good bosses as well colleagues mostly ask you the same question
Each time you meet
"How are you?"
And the only answer you find is:
"I am fine thank you"
Even if you are close to suicide at the moment
But it's good at least they don't have to listen your thoughts
That are.. well let's say messy at times
So all is fine

Just a bit rainy perhaps

Resignation

Now I don't need to hurt you nor do anything else
It's time to simply live like nothing happen
It's not a first time like this and well
There is really nothing to fight for

So

Let's move on

Losing name

Don't call yourself my man
My man wouldn't do it to me again
You lost this privilege

You are free now
Enjoy your time

The point is that in the particular case and in this stage of life
I do no longer wished to dream only
I have been doing this for years and suddenly I needed some change
That I shouldn't..perhaps I know but...sometimes we need this
So now some dreams are only a step away from the actions I wish to make..and I do
In to the right direction that follows my needs but of course anything ever in life
Is not so easy nor so clear
And our steps should come naturally sometimes accidentally, just in time too, if they don't
All seems ruined and not worth to try to go for anymore
But these are emotions we can't always hide nor erase
Especially standing face to face
With these we wish to be perfectly real with
So all goes wrong at times
And there is nowhere to go after all
Nor even dreams stay in you
Except some of this we still feel inside
The regrets, and thoughts, some decisions that we make
Each day seems so different this way
Life flows with all its surprises again
To give us new inspiration and terms to come with
Here or there well it all just flows away
Nothing is stable, nothing will remain
Just these few feelings inside
Few broken dreams, few scars and some good memories too
Oh life, there is still so much ahead
There is also an experience behind
And this is what is all about
In fact

Life and dreams

And you
You just hurt by this never ending fake you make
You are just a bigger dreamer than I
That's why
We can't fit right
Even if all seems so sweet at times
In a dream land
You helped me to create
Once upon a time
It's nothing but a tell story
And well
It came to end
When I wakened up again

I tried so hard
To catch the dream
Like it was real
You are nothing but a rain drop
And the charm splash
When I try to have you for real
Then you disappear
And
Tears remain

That's how it is with you
And this life and dreams too

I was silly again
How silly I was
I am afraid...
Too bad

Little thing

When there is not much to gain
There is not much to lose as well
So you live your life as it was before
Just without

From other hand

But if all these sweet little things
Make you happy
There is neither way nor sense to leave
In fact they are all
What you really enjoy and have...
All the rest is just a waste
An exaggeration the form over the content
Or selfishness and expectations over the love, so

Let's enjoy the moment
When it comes
And let's wait for more of them
Always
With the same hope
Because we know
That it works
And that it is
Just exactly this
What we want
Both
Still

Let it be
As it is

Yes

Dear reader I hope you enjoyed this little trip through mind creations it is just another day or few in the world of dreams mixed with reality of every day life, some special moments worth to remember..I hope this may reflex some moments in you so we go hand in hand in space smiling like we know a very special secret that only few really discovered so far..

To be continued...

Best regards

Anna Cellmer

www.ingramcontent.com/pod-product-compliance
Lightning Source LLC
Chambersburg PA
CBHW021011090426
42738CB00007B/753